Too Cute!
Baby Koalas

by Rebecca Sabelko

BELLWETHER MEDIA
MINNEAPOLIS, MN

Blastoff! Beginners are developed by literacy experts and educators to meet the needs of early readers. These engaging informational texts support young children as they begin reading about their world. Through simple language and high frequency words paired with crisp, colorful photos, Blastoff! Beginners launch young readers into the universe of independent reading.

Sight Words in This Book

a	eat	one	this
all	in	out	up
are	is	ride	
at	like	the	
big	look	then	
by	on	they	

This edition first published in 2022 by Bellwether Media, Inc.

No part of this publication may be reproduced in whole or in part without written permission of the publisher. For information regarding permission, write to Bellwether Media, Inc., Attention: Permissions Department, 6012 Blue Circle Drive, Minnetonka, MN 55343.

Library of Congress Cataloging-in-Publication Data

Names: Sabelko, Rebecca, author.
Title: Baby koalas / Rebecca Sabelko.
Description: Minneapolis, MN : Bellwether Media, 2022. | Series: Too cute! | Includes bibliographical references and index. | Audience: Ages 4-7 | Audience: Grades K-1
Identifiers: LCCN 2021040727 (print) | LCCN 2021040728 (ebook) | ISBN 9781644875759 (library binding) | ISBN 9781648345869 (ebook)
Subjects: LCSH: Koala--Infancy--Juvenile literature.
Classification: LCC QL737.M384 S23 2022 (print) | LCC QL737.M384 (ebook) | DDC 599.2/51392--dc23
LC record available at https://lccn.loc.gov/2021040727
LC ebook record available at https://lccn.loc.gov/2021040728

Text copyright © 2022 by Bellwether Media, Inc. BLASTOFF! BEGINNERS and associated logos are trademarks and/or registered trademarks of Bellwether Media, Inc.

Editor: Amy McDonald   Designer: Jeffrey Kollock

Printed in the United States of America, North Mankato, MN.

Table of Contents

A Baby Koala!	4
In the Pouch	6
Out of the Pouch	10
All Grown Up!	20
Baby Koala Facts	22
Glossary	23
To Learn More	24
Index	24

A Baby Koala!

Look at the baby koala.
Hello, joey!

joey

In the Pouch

Newborn joeys are very small. They grow in mom's **pouch**.

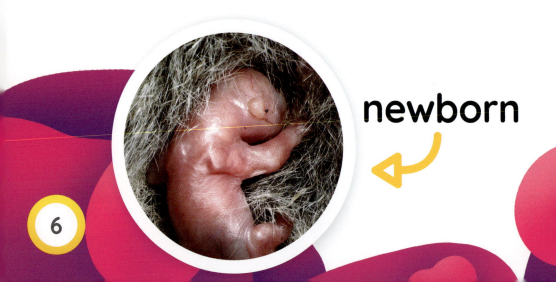

newborn

Joeys **nurse**.
They grow big.
Then they
peek out.

Out of the Pouch

Joeys leave the pouch. They stay by mom.

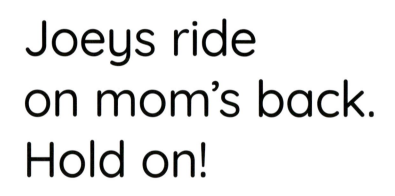

Joeys ride
on mom's back.
Hold on!

Joeys climb trees. This one is up high!

Joeys sleep a lot.
They nap in trees.

Joeys eat at night. They like leaves.

All Grown Up!

This joey is
all grown up.
Goodbye, mom!

Baby Koala Facts

Koala Life Stages

newborn   joey   adult

A Day in the Life

ride on mom   climb trees   eat leaves

Glossary

just born

to drink mom's milk

a pocket on the belly of a mother koala

To Learn More

ON THE WEB

FACTSURFER

Factsurfer.com gives you a safe, fun way to find more information.

1. Go to www.factsurfer.com.

2. Enter "baby koalas" into the search box and click 🔍.

3. Select your book cover to see a list of related content.

Index

climb, 14
eat, 18
grow, 6, 8, 20
koala, 4
leaves, 18
mom, 6, 10, 11, 12, 20
nap, 16
newborn, 6
night, 18
nurse, 8
peek, 8
pouch, 6, 10
ride, 12
sleep, 16
trees, 14, 16

The images in this book are reproduced through the courtesy of: apple2499, front cover; Eric Isselee, pp. 3, 4, 5, 13, 22 (adult); D. Parer & E. Parer-Cook, pp. 6, 22 (newborn), 23 (newborn); Suzi Eszterhas, pp. 6-7, 8-9, 23 (pouch); Yori Hirokawa, pp. 10-11; Benjamint, p. 12; Andras Deak, pp. 14-15, 22 (climb); worldswildlifewonders, pp. 16-17; Scisetti Alfio, p. 18; dangdumrong, pp. 18-19, 22 (eat); Thorsten Spoerlein, pp. 20-21; Animal Search, p. 22 (joey); Constantin Stanciu, p. 22 (ride on mom); Rashid Valitov, p. 23 (nurse).